Nathan Walker

Condensations

Uniformbooks 2017

*for Frank Townsley Walker
aka 'Wuky'*

First published 2017
Copyright © Nathan Walker
ISBN 978-1-910010-14-3

Uniformbooks
7 Hillhead Terrace, Axminster, Devon EX13 5JL
www.uniformbooks.co.uk

Trade distribution in the UK by Central Books
www.centralbooks.com

Printed and bound by T J International, Padstow, Cornwall

CONDENSATIONS

Contents

Preface	7
1. *Says*	9
2. *Long*	31
3. *Walk*	47
4. *A Bran New Wuk*	65
Sources & Acknowledgements	71
APP. *Ambl*	73

CONDENSATIONS

Preface

In June 2016 I was writer in residence at the Armitt Museum and Library in Ambleside, Cumbria. The writing I encountered and completed there forms the following 'condensations'.

The texts are constructed by erasing material from pages of books and manuscripts from the Armitt library and archives and superimposing these partially erased pages. These treatments arrange writing on the following subjects: the history of rock climbing in the Lake District; Cumbrian (Cumberland and Westmorland) dialect; the industrial heritage of Cumbria; Westmorland mythology and rituals; and texts by and about cultural figures in Cumbrian history including exiled German artist Kurt Schwitters, mountaineer and magician Aleister Crowley and the historian T. W. Thompson.

These texts have been collaged and written through with my own original writing, West Cumbrian place-names and transcribed conversations with my paternal grandfather ('Wuky') on his life on the mountains and specifically his experience of building a cairn on Knock Murton and a wall in his kitchen in West Cumbria.

1

Says

loss   organised
                     the spot

                                 jaw moota

form behind. Our task
grand.   the Rock
             pressed

        Never drop burn

                              The building
                               of the
                              gritstone furnace
    Low   first
    little book   placements
        absence out   instruments
                              technique

            brothers leadings
            dialect speaking
               handsome

                    witness my hand
                           a linguistic atlas

                                         suitable intona

         lexicalnest
           subsiding

have broke down and quite before us
mountain
have to wait till the
says

man
    dressingdug   Lakes red disfiguration
                             low recording
                          we hugful face

                                    short as their say wuz

                    thirsting
                    parallel
              whether repast wallets
                      grapes
    scant attention shape
         his table
              itch of
         climbs   on the desert slabs
         The written word as not   hard
              Head

                                        north

sing ~~out and raise~~ ~~fled walkers~~
these places within

the wording
rope,

Theworkdoesconvert the word. Is the bound hem
      way
vent

                              Buttresses were
                              used elsewhere.
                       steep bank
                       the Fadther
            sandstone   house-fast
foundcaughtapparentlyrdle
                        firmly

                                    ~~Stone~~
                                    ~~spirits~~
                              to do   so

                           actual words
                                    Longland

              fields~~cowshouse~~~~crackface~~
                  ~~low~~   ~~through~~
                 bloomsmithies .rest
                      legen~~dary~~ ~~in~~accessibility
            encircling fires   ~~other doings~~
                            climb laycrag

their remains are sound

fore set m charcoal would be to top knock

                                        quite   the house
                                                                        re-built
            seedless pacing   area

                                                            kinds of notions
                                                            bearing

standing   and gather

                The figures
        We always refer

                    sheepcotes
                       ladies
                      & heads & mouths
                    praises all several
                his brother estate in Trisdale
                          fair cry
                       abandoned
                      a poor name arisen

                                         Pisgah
              arose, or has since arisen   ask
                                          reaches
                           spoke Rib and Slab
                               refers to land
                              to drown
                  never been repeated
                  for exploration

                    forges
tent fiel̶d̶ ̶w̶o̶r̶k̶i̶n̶g̶ climb are left unsung
    f̶a̶c̶e̶ ̶o̶f̶ ̶t̶h̶a̶t̶ ̶m̶o̶u̶n̶t̶a̶i̶n̶
wanted to ex̶p̶a̶n̶s̶i̶v̶e̶ ̶l̶a̶c̶e̶ ̶   ning t̶o̶ ̶m̶a̶d̶e̶
              r̶e̶a̶l̶l̶y̶ ̶b̶e̶g̶i̶n̶   Pinnacle

                        No oak a̶ ̶c̶o̶h̶e̶r̶e̶n̶t̶ material disrupting
                                s̶u̶p̶e̶r̶f̶i̶n̶e̶

North and fissures-West
warps

quently usual
then
  fall the man   apart neglect the other crags
    Nape   boundless that give us wool

preserving concrete   Both being
   P Wright in Cumberland, West
    nought   Shmabertha

                                    nivver 'ad yan

What's the BARN for water-lifts great object
in the barn undermentioned wood-leave
hold rain leaf sheets plethora and severity
formation fire sheets next to place
overlapping phase

                    the Neppbbishenfengaged in working
Watshocaloned cliffs had been
   sister   swept clean

  barren

                                            left-hand
                                       virgin crag
                           here in these parts
                    At a remote dygg

           Dow
           furnaces
Man   truely important alienation
      in I carried
   abandoned charcoal

            eye for a routine
         quite sick chimney period
      bodies steep rocks   led
         Nor' roves'
         Nor'
      locality
      backbarrow along athletic indulgent
         The langabout newshead
         Plain Furness with   Ark
                    I got together
                 Pave alphabet
                      title
                   down
            scrap

2
Long

escarping The rage widpohshedistoherhand
                                    LowhiteCircles
                      foaming
   Ullswaterfelles pity of the belts
        Bannererfelles   Shoessworth
               flurries

      behind Helvellyst summer
            heart   adultsavage
              mound
           ring   made out
             cups Harrington No
         pressure of earth
        arisenfairnessng bundles habit
      holdsaidede
  Cumbriaarea suffused clearswarth

                    Wether scarping
         word
   cloudclasped
        bundles
         absence
           said

                              lake   Megling and stands
                              drypendingng
                              cavity

                fold

  glacial action

                                                    mark
                                                    voices

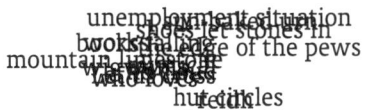
unemployment situation
books ice stones in
mountain edge of the pews
hut tents
circles

land juts
nearly true walkers
north

knoll

solid rock rough
earthen barrow

draining of the land
a halt is made
still carried into the building

Table sea
objects

beds

decade such labour
sweeps its has coastal
          meet inclosed

                                        soil less
                                     hand
                                         wet

                                                                        districts
                                                                         scored
                                                                         circle

                                    name

                            border
                             arrangement
                              speech
                     heather till of the
                              the lake
                            pits   heapbeacon
                       surface

                    and her Daughters
              Knock
        like a friend   strewing the floor
                                                together met
                                                 brother

                              long
                                      constellations

        camp
  priestronghold s   we have tit each may be built
      Samaria   aroused in the distance
       slope   herd
                                        vicinity
                 Opium is the Walking language—it never dies
                      the old trains
                  makes something more
                       moss and flowers
                         stony
                      unpolished stone

deeply considered houses while floors were of refuse Hartsop
           those ages   mountains

                    ink

              the lake and   the dead

                        w

tone

ear
slabs

soundlace
working plands ight assister
have been removed more is dining stone Circles
unhewn ried solemnity
torn lasa neighbourhood
lip appendages
 penetrating
mouth art scenes

             as impassable girl
        rustic ceremonies and
           rarely border
                  gathered from the lake
        lads seams were too thin and dirty
        felts, roping silent
                   obsolete

                 typical
        remains people at the wakes   spoils strike
               stocks water of carrying them
                   one lay   last timber

                              lying justify
                                 neatly
                             fading shore
        poeticised is by seating a que present the oldest
                                measurements
                             I was present
                                   name

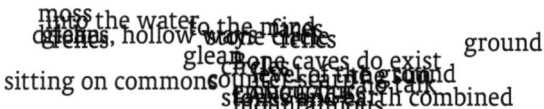
moss the water the minds
ditches, hollow stone ditches ground
gleam one caves do exist
sitting on commons of these soaring sound
strange mouth combined
mountainous

                   standing flag   Workington
      copstone

                                                  frowns

 cloud circle
appendages, to which I have given place

maen

.

  men

                                    map adorn
                                break the brake
                            materials have been removed
                                                 preparation plant
                               the water of the mound
                        smaller stones   furnaces
                                 the overspillswater
                                                    elbowscape

                                          by the
                                       memory   ringer in
                                 vast
                                           morass   district
                                     blocks of stone
                                                    this stone

        remains softness   favor   intimacy with air
             dust   ramparts near to   veined peeled
               calm short cuts ascends
            bounded A rain in inkers ribbons
           boulders kinds hung line of stones
                 north
            much larger

                          tops

.

land

habitants
workingconditions   they are at sea
remaining
mound
locality

scrap

3

Walk

pass drawn

correcting and ~~amplifying~~ vernacular speech. Further, or sentences and all the tree   volumes

                          In much of this difficulty
                          void of all effort
                          My might en

                weatherclaw
                      attention on the rock
                                         holdless
           edges or ribs
                 toughness

                    bant ab li
                    pout le lit
              intact
              At the end
   procedure

   ploughing

                              pulling up and down

                              the whole book

Flare   tape

                    hear
              documents
    cutting

                         the top
          discordant   Brocken
                  cow with painted
                   linear desk stairs
                         landscape muscles
            stacking
                         Crag. The second

A postal
                             Cultivation
                         full
                      forcing
                 losses

                                    recorder ready
                                           Body

         clumsy in cracks

              Pillar Stone
                          stand
         sharpened
              enabled him and work
                        action
                   to crack

.

                    loppings croppings and bruisings men
                                        class
              in the plot hologi Mbst ape naming
                        few grounds
                        solitary

                              cryptic ft rope
                                    detail doleborder
                                 greater care
                                          air industries
on to   almost slab   our projected Atlas. This
                   crags oet   trouble
                              Broad
                                                                letter

                         slab and wall period

n**ditch**c**raft**
     not of eventual deposit
        derived
              Instead

                              stroke

there was nothing I have heard
throw light on his body
　　　　open work
　　landing on sound
　　　fell in

just

abandonmenssable hills
to retire it
What do you call this? hair

         humble handmaid
          held whom we
       end of Pikes
              sake
              neophyte

mendous

                                                  a dagger

and ~~to iron~~

rock-starvation

                                    Plain Furness
         ing a new technique browse the toppings
                  Wordsworth from
            land raddles

~~TEETH~~ ly   climbs are short
~~carefully~~melting

                                    suitably spaced

                                    ridden

Saws knee rain wilt days

Napes. The last seven scalp are orschooling?

Atlas

Fell a Rock climbing Naomi
marriage speaking
these days peeling
Needle bearing

4

A Bran New Wuk

                    tickle thear
            naa
                        lang
       nivver border
          Do well fawking
    wandering wept   dufting maufe
     rubbing break a what nivver named
   lang trok lockerkill a bonney
    leak to yans feet   deaf ear
   ditywhak at them thin
        wh knaw   memory
      mak naa warte
    naa maaledan mild breia for
   toash weats bander flown
        them up   afk
          where as with a tongue
       nowhere at yankegrown
         tongue

                          transfer aloft at ivvery
                          twisten   bad ward
                               girls give
                       They nivver cou'd du it
                               Mere
                              maak flowly
                     folks prawling wolf
                       gang wrang
                            I only annex fuch

                          wild

                              the act of growing
                     dry as kiln-fryaks
                           drop dawn
                     aur wooning is net
                                   mare

                                mun
                         this varra neet

                                                            knocking on the head

            yan comes   kept
        bodies alone   rattle end
            fleep grown haw
          knaws   Hood
           they wad play wi Craw
         thefe knots and barrows
              fenca wayworn
           Invery baut a hang
           the all day holding
           brokken
           black raindle tree

                moving flawly a voice that wad carry a league
                cry aut fro Woodland sae lood my luve all our ideas
                fen I   the all   tkins oor
                and   bran new
                in clauted terms, net that my remarks of
                         alaan yaw droon ahoch of fears
            what rhaading   treads
                 winder   fildion on braut

                    bauk and
                     fiery comet
            a body none of fuffered
                    body one
                    sleeen

                      placed

              yet le me met with
                    love his brother

                          aur fadthur's
                hev the means
                    and prevent

              wrap raund the ancles
                        falls

                            body dea
                          wad

                        teata

                                        bodies

        hev oready
          barn tea
            repeats
          lay
        wha hey
            marrows another
              give and tak
                 an chelow
          lad threw books
        folks hev been
        young trees ea net
                 nut the fadthurlefs
              for my books
            laa kind onthe ords
               inleght werks
                 in this
              walked wad be
              foa far fra
            leeve in caves and holes
                 fliam to lee
        werds to my pafs for a witch
              dirty mary flerks
               ftane-walls
                  wuks

                    tune
    awn   rain
        he nivver
     rougher   fra crag
       barn
              dogs
    may it du foa when

                    we his arms
                   ye leak dew fog
                    let us enter foame,
         heard   binding on
                     haw life meets them
            baneing   rags
                                      copy tone vance and
                                       burn rather yoaks that
                                       wabare ebbgowmoon
                                         a whis thee   fpeak

           tender clerk if
             claps   fadthurs and brethren
           amang father   poor   a piece
                           er fent for   as ufu blead
                           years knees   bund
              ftarving   the
              DRUNKARD   talk thefe
                          huivver   leakssaa

                              'tother
                              heckvoice

                amang   wha
                 of days

          body mud

                      neak ta

Sources

Arp, H., Schwitters, K., Klee, P., trans. Watts, H. *Three painter-poets, Arp, Schwitters, Klee: Selected poems*. Harmondsworth: Penguin, 1974.

Burton, A. *Rush-bearing: An account of the old custom of strewing rushes: Carrying rushes to church; the rush-cart; garlands in churches; morris-dancers; the wakes; the rush*. Manchester: Brook & Chrystal, 1891.

Cooper, C. J. A. *Great Gable*. Ulverston: Fell and Rock Climbing Club of the English Lake District, 1937.

Crowley, A. *Clouds without water: Edited from a private M.S.* London: Privately printed for circulation among ministers of religion, 1909.

Daysh, G. H. J. *West Cumberland (with Alston) a survey of industrial facilities*. Whitehaven: Cumberland Development Council, 1938.

Denwood, M. & Thompson, T. W. *A Lafter o' Farleys in t' dialects o' Lakeland, 1760–1945*. Carlisle: Lakeland Dialect Society, 1950.

Ellwood, T. *Lakeland and Iceland, being a glossary of words in the dialect of Cumberland, Westmoreland and North Lancashire which seem allied to or identical with the Icelandic or Norse, together with cognate placenames and surnames, and a supplement of words used in shepherding, folk-lore and antiquities*. London: The English Dialect Society, 1895.

Hedevind, B. 'Scandinavian elements in the dialect and place names of Dent on the West Riding of Yorkshire'. Paper presented at the Annual General Meeting of the Society of Leeds, 25th May 1957. Yorkshire Dialect Society, 1959.

Hodge, A. V. *'Pig trade' A dialogue in the Cumberland and Scottish border dialect*. Carlisle: Chas. Thurnam & Sons, 1909.

Housman, J. *A descriptive tour, and guide to the lakes, caves, mountains, and other natural curiosities, in Cumberland, Westmoreland, Lancashire, and a part of the West Riding of Yorkshire*. Carlisle: Printed by F. Jollie, 1808.

Hutton, W. *A bran new wark, by William de Worfat, containing a true calendar of his thoughts concerning good nebberhood. Naw first printed fra his M.S. for the use of the hamlet of Woodland*. Kendal: Printed by W. Pennington, 1785.

Orton, H. *Atlas linguistiques: Linguistic atlas of England*. Orbis Vol.9, 1960. pp.331–348.

Rice, H. A. L. *Curiosities of Lakeland*. Newcastle upon Tyne: Frank Graham, 1974.

Sansom, G. S. *Climbing at Wasdale before the First World War*. Castle Cary: Castle Cary Press, 1982.

Schwitters, K. *Das literarische werk*. Köln: DuMont Schauberg, 1973.

Sidgwick, A. H. *Walking essays*. London: E. Arnold, 1912.

Taylor, M. W. 'On the vestiges of Celtic occupation near Ullswater, and so the discovery of buried stone circles by Eamont Side'. In *Transactions of the Cumberland and Westmorland Antiquarian & Archæological Society*, Vol.1 1866–67. Kendal: Cumberland and Westmorland Antiquarian and Archaeological Society. Printed by T. Wilson and Sons, 1870.

Thompson, T. W. 'Fred. T. Robinson to T. W. Thompson. November 25, 1947'. [Armitt Ref: ALMS 166: 38ii]. Note: Correspondence relating to 'A Lafter o' Farley's' and the correct spelling of the word Father as 'Fadther' not 'Fatther'.

Whaley, D., & English Place-Name Society. *A dictionary of Lake District place-names*. Nottingham: English Place-Name Society, 2006.

Wilson, T. W. *'Childer' studies in the Westmorland dialect*, No.2. Kendal: T. Wilson, 1898.

Acknowledgements

Heartfelt thanks to Deborah Walsh at the Armitt Museum for her generosity and wisdom throughout the project. Thanks also to the Armitt Staff, especially Sue. I am grateful to Scott Thurston for considered thoughts and conversations. Thank you to Victoria Kent Gray for our walks and her unfaltering encouragment. This project was supported by the Armitt Museum & Gallery, using public funding by the National Lottery through Arts Council England and research funding from York St John University.

APPENDIX

Ambl

Ambl is a series of performance actions for camera made in the Armitt Museum and surrounding landscape of Ambleside. These were quiet interventions. Similar to the processes explored in *Condensations*, these actions applied strategies of superimposition, juxtaposition and reduction to create temporary landscapes. The camera took four timed exposures over a one-minute duration, two frames from each performance are reproduced here.

How Head Barn, Ambleside

Armitt Library

Armitt Museum, Kurt Schwitters Exhibit

Grasmere

Helm Cragg

Loughrigg Fell